TIERS OF HEALING II

Self Guided Workbook...Journey To Acceptance

by

ANNE BROWNING

ISBN: 097715033X

ISBN-13: 9780977150335

Library of Congress Control Number: 2013909149
CreateSpace Independent Publishing Platform
North Charleston, SC

TIERS OF HEALING
OVERVIEW & WELCOME

Welcome to Tiers of Healing. We have been where you are. Each of us has suffered great loss, has grieved, and has had thoughts that life would never be good again. Life will be good again. If we were able to move from a place of hopelessness and despair to a place where there was a glimmer of hope, we know you will be able to do the same. If we were able to build on that hope and find a grudging sense of acceptance for all that was lost to us, we know that you will also be able to do the same. If each of us was able to find a new vision for what would one day become our new normal, we are certain it is possible for you. Finally, if we—with little support—were able to take the steps to reach that vision and live a full and joyful life, we know you will have the ability to take those steps as well. We are here to support you.

The Tiers of Healing program was originally designed to be facilitated in small groups. That product is still available, and there are groups that meet to move through all the tiers of loss together, finding hope and friendship along the way. The book you have purchased has many of the components of our group program but is designed for individual study. We urge you to find someone to share your journey with, perhaps a trusted friend, mentor, or coach. We welcome your sharing through anne@tiersofhealing.com.

To make the most of this material, allow the gift of time. Healing loss is possible if you decide to do the work that is required. The amount of time will vary with each individual—a maximum of three hours a day and a minimum of forty minutes is a good place to begin. Know that you are not alone. The exercises in these workbooks are not difficult, yet they can be profound and must be assimilated to move forward.

Find a quiet place and consecrate it for your healing. Bless the space, perhaps adding flowers or meaningful mementos. You will need a place to write and writing materials. Some exercises ask you to have crayons or perhaps paper plates. Please note the supplies needed at the start of each session.

A session takes approximately ten to fifteen minutes to read (some may be longer) and anywhere from fifteen to thirty minutes to complete the exercises. All sessions have a music suggestion; you may use the suggestion provided or find your own music. We strongly urge you to include music in your healing journey.

We have included a Weather Report Chart. This is an important tool, and we urge you to copy it and keep it in a place where you can make notes daily. Very often during times of loss and chaos, we feel as if we are making no progress. The weather report is an excellent tool to note those days that were sunny and to also aid you in noting what it was you did or what you were thinking that helped make the day sunny. Equally, it can be a great way to note if you are in a place where day after day, week after week, you appear to be getting worse. We urge each of you to care for yourself and to seek professional help in addition to this self-help guide. It may take a village to raise a child, but it takes an army to heal a loss.

We celebrate your courage. Loss must be healed. It has a way of hiding deep within the soul, robbing us of energy, joy, and motivation. Sometimes we believe we have "gotten past it," yet, as we view the world, we are easily angered, tire more quickly, or just see the world as a place of dreary sameness. Once the hurt is healed, the joy in living returns, and life once again becomes hopeful.

At no time do we tell you that the journey is not painful. It is. At no time do we tell you that you will stop missing what you've lost. You won't. At no time do we tell you that life will be like it used to be. It will not. What we will tell you is pain comes to us all; misery, however, is a choice, and you can choose to opt out of it. What we will tell you is there is always something to miss as you grow, yet there can be smiles and laughter and joyful memories, not only longing. Finally, we will tell you that you do not know what lies ahead. Life has changed; there will be more joys, more laughter, more love, and it will be different than it was. It will be your new normal, and you may like it. There is at least hope that you will one day be on the other side of your loss, and you will be OK. We know—we have traveled the path, and we are OK. Most days, we are better than OK.

Welcome. We are here for you and with you.

Contact info:
anne@tiersofhealing.com

ACKNOWLEDGMENTS

Tiers of Healing Self-Study Guides are based on a program Linda Debelser Owen and I created. The four-part program is designed for small groups. Tiers of Healing for groups, was and continues to be, a mission of love for both Linda and myself. I owe a deep thanks to Linda for her vision, her dedication, and most importantly, her friendship.

There were months and months of talks, writing, rewriting, editing and more editing and rewriting. Not once did I hear Linda complain about the work involved. She kept her eye on her vision of reaching hurting people and helping them heal. Linda lives in Canada and runs the Canadian Tiers program. She has delivered the group material to churches, women fighting breast cancer, indigenous people who are still recovering from land loss and she is the woman I turn to when I need a laugh, a push or a strong shoulder. She is my hero. I acknowledge her expertise, her commitment, her integrity and her love.

I want to acknowledge all the men, women and children who have had a loss and continue to live their lives fully and who have the compassion to reach out to others who are in pain. I acknowledge those to whom this book is dedicated, individuals who are in pain and feel alone. I assure you, you are *not* alone.

We are here and we have known your pain.

Donna Lipman, of Austin, Texas, is the woman who recorded the DVD portion of the Tiers of Healing for Groups. She is a woman of deep compassion, brilliant insights. Her commitment to filling our world with peace and joy was begun at birth. Everyone adores Donna. She has delivered the Tiers for Groups in Austin and she used the material in a very real way when her husband, Terry Lipman, who did the filming for the DVD, died suddenly. I acknowledge her, love her and treasure her friendship.

My husband, Peter Schroeder, helped Linda and I with the editing and reading of Tiers of Healing for Groups. He was instrumental in getting the Tiers of Healing Self Study Guides completed and is editing Tiers of Helping and Tiers of Hope. Peter is the miracle that God sent to me as answered prayer in 1988. He continues to inspire me, strengthen me, hold me and without him my life would be much less bright. I love you, Peter.

Finally, I must acknowledge my mentor, teacher and friend, Debbie Ford. Thank you, Debbie for your work, your guidance, your love.

TIERS OF HEALING
TIER II: JOURNEY TO ACCEPTANCE
Self-Guided Workbook II

TABLE OF CONTENTS

TIERS OF HEALING II
SESSION 1: SELF-CARE REVIEW

It's a funny thing about life. If you refuse to settle for anything less than the best, that's what it will give you.—W. Somerset Maugham

Music Suggestion: "The Flower That Shattered the Stone" by John Denver

Tier II is about the start of accepting the unacceptable. This is an ongoing life process, and acceptance concerning a loss can be very difficult. Acceptance may be difficult, but it is mandatory for healing. The longer you stand in a place of refusing to accept your loss, the greater your pain and the more difficult your future. Let us remind you that acceptance does not mean what happened was right, good, or fair. You need not like what has happened; in fact, you may still actively hate the situation you find yourself in. All you need is to accept that you are here, and you have had a loss.

In this session we will present ways to look at your loss that may make it easier to accept. We will continue with how to deal with anger, as begun in Tier I and introduce forgiveness. Struggle is an option, and many find themselves locked in a circle of struggle when there is a way to move beyond the struggle. We will give you some ideas for coping with struggle. This is an important session and vital to creating a new vision for your life and the lives of those you love. Before you can begin to dive into what acceptance is and if it is possible for you, we must first review your Self-Care Contract. We have included another Contract in this book. Please make copies of it and update your Contract periodically. Act with integrity, and keep your word to care for yourself.

If you read and did the exercises in Tier I ("Journey through Grief"), you will already have an Acknowledgment Box. You may want to add self-acknowledgment to your Self-Care Contract. Challenge yourself and increase your care. You will notice that as you choose to care for yourself, you will be making a statement to the universe and to yourself that you are worth caring for. As stated in Tier I, healing from a loss requires an enormous amount of energy, and it may be some of the toughest work you have ever done. Be certain you are in top shape to do this work and follow your Self-Care Contract.

SELF – CARE CONTRACT

I, _____, commit myself to the following self-care, beginning this week. (List here what you will actually do. Make sure this is a realistic and measurable plan.)

_____

_____

_____

_____

_____

_____

_____

_____

_____

I will begin working on self-care _____ for _____

                               DATE   **LENGTH OF TIME**

When I achieve this goal, I will award myself with:

I will evaluate the achievement of this goal with my support person. (Be certain to find someone who will hold you accountable to this contract.)

    Name: _____

    Date: _____

    Contacted by: _____ (How will you contact your support person? Phone, e-mail, in person.)

Signed: _____

Support person: _____ Date: _____

Exercises: Session 1

Supplies Needed: Self-Care Contract, Pen or Markers, Acknowledgment Box, Journal or Paper

1. Create a place for your "inner work": A place to listen to or to read uplifting words. Be sure it is a place you enjoy, and it is free of clutter.
2. Fill out your Self-Care Contract and place it where you will see it daily. Be certain to have a person you can check in with who will hold you accountable.
3. If you do not have an Acknowledgment Box, buy, make, or find a beautiful box and place those items that hold great meaning for you inside. These are items that speak of an accomplishment or milestone in your life. They may be photos, certificates, thank-you cards, or news clippings. Add to the box on a regular basis.
4. Begin to track three successes and three challenges you face each week and what behaviors, thoughts, or beliefs supported them during the week. Write these in your journal weekly, or keep track in some other manner.

TIERS OF HEALING II
SESSION 2: COST OF STRUGGLE

God grant me the serenity
To accept the things I cannot change,
The courage to change the things I can,
And the wisdom to know the difference.
—The Serenity Prayer

Music Suggestion: "The Great Pretender" by The Platters

The days go by, and more and more, we find ourselves struggling to find answers to questions that need no answers or have no answers. We swim in an ocean of information too deep for us to decipher, struggling to sift through it so we can add meaning to our lives. While drowning in the struggle, we miss the rainbow, the caress of the wind, the song of the bird, and the laughter waiting to be heard in our own souls.

Struggle occurs when we resist what is. Every cell in our body screams, "It cannot be so!" but it is. We push away from that which sickens us, pains us, and has robbed us of a life in which we were comfortable and possibly loved. Everything you believed your life to be has now changed, and we are inviting you to accept what is. Anger may surface, saying the words, "You have no idea of what I have lost." We do know. We have been there. We also struggled. We also raged. The struggle caused us additional pain and kept us locked in a battle we could never win. Once we accepted what was, regardless of our feelings, we began the long journey back to a life of joy and passion. There is hope.

In Eastern martial arts, there is a technique you can use to disable your opponent. When an opponent grabs onto you, your first reaction is to pull away. In martial arts, you are shown how to go into the pull. Try this experiment: find a friend or family member and ask him or her to pull on your arm. Now, pull back, and notice that the other person will pull even harder. You may eventually get free, but it will require a great deal of effort. Now ask your friend to pull on your arm, and this time, go with the pull. Your friend will in all likelihood let go or make it easier for you to slip out of his or her grasp.

Life is like the pull. Go with what life has given you, and you will find ways to break free of the pain or learn new ways to succeed.

Loss can create a sense of being overwhelmed. If you are too hungry, too tired, too angry, or too lonely, you will fall easily into the struggle of accepting the unacceptable. It is very important that you monitor your physical and emotional needs. Be certain you are eating healthy meals, getting adequate rest, releasing your anger in healthy, productive ways, and calling on family and friends to visit. It is your responsibility to care for yourself.

Very often what we struggle with most is what we have made our loss mean. A loss is bad enough without adding drama and doom to what has happened. Note the facts of what has happened in your life (for example, your wife has died), and then note what you have decided this means (I will be alone the rest of my life; I will never find another woman I can love; I will never heal this hole in my heart). The loss of a spouse is indeed cataclysmic and takes a great deal of work to heal. You may always have a part of you that will miss her, but that does *not mean* you will be alone forever, you will never find love again, or you will never heal. It is easy to believe this drama in the early stages of grief and loss, but it is important to begin to challenge that which is not 100 percent true as you move forward in your healing. When we love, the love stays, but our hearts are beautiful, and there is always room for more love. Always.

You may not want to give up the struggle. You may not believe that the struggle creates only more pain and suffering. You may decide to hold onto your loss. What we ask is that you be *willing* to be *willing*. Say to yourself, "I am willing to be willing to let go of my struggle."

Often, just *noticing* that you are involved in a struggle begins the process of releasing the struggle.

Exercises: Session 2

Supplies Needed: Journal or paper and pen

1. Make a list of the things you still resist about your situation.
2. What situations do you struggle with the most?
3. Which limiting thoughts do you most often struggle to keep away?
4. What causes you to become overwhelmed?
5. When are you most vulnerable to becoming overwhelmed?
6. Make a list of what your struggle costs you (for example, money, tears, sleepless nights, regret, etc.)
7. Ask yourself what is the biggest struggle you are experiencing, and ask yourself who could help you move out of the struggle.

TIERS OF HEALING II
SESSION 3: ANGER

Unresolved anger is often the hidden source of low self-esteem.
—Bill Barlow

Music Suggestion: Find a good loud piece of music.

In Tier I we began the discussion of anger: the different styles it takes, how to get in touch with anger, and how to express anger in a healthy way. In Tier 2, we will be exploring this emotion on a different level.

Many types of energy exist in our world. We have atomic energy, electrical energy, wind energy, intellectual energy, and many other kinds as well. Each kind of energy has a specific and helpful use. What happens when that energy gets trapped, blocked, or stored up? In some cases, it explodes and causes great damage. In other cases, if it is not used, it dissipates and is wasted. When handled and used properly, all energy may be used for the good of humanity.

Just like in the cases above, our anger can be used to cause great damage, or it can be used for the greater good of all. How you handle your anger and in which circumstances you use it will determine whether or not it will cause damage or be used for the greater good.

Anger left unexpressed will grow like a volcano until it erupts. Talking out anger is like a relief valve that keeps us from exploding. Hurt that has been denied, mislabeled, or unrecognized still exists, no matter how long ago we were wounded. When we bury our collection of hurts, abuses, losses, and fears, they turn into anger and seep out through our cracks. In some cases, the seeping becomes a flood, which, if left unchecked, becomes what is perceived as a "normal" state of being. This leads us to become people who are always angry, hostile, defensive, and forever operating with a short fuse. We can blow up in people's faces without even knowing what set us off.

Another problem with burying our anger is that it will eat us from the inside. Buried anger can lead to a host of physical ailments. Anger turned inward can lead to depression. If this sounds familiar to you, you need to turn that anger out or see a therapist who can help you dispel some of this buried anger.

For now, try to get in touch with the things that make you angry. What are your pet peeves? What could be underneath your anger? Very often, anger is the tip of many softer emotions that are painful to express—emotions such as sadness, grief, shame, guilt, low self-esteem, or loneliness. If you can find and express these softer emotions, the anger will dissolve. It is much like an iceberg: what you see above the water is only a small part of the iceberg. The largest part of an iceberg is below the water line and cannot be seen. If you truly want to dissolve an iceberg, you must melt what is below the surface and not concentrate on what is above the surface.

Exercises: Session 3

Supplies Needed: white paper, crayons, and a pen.

1. Draw an iceberg on a piece of white paper. Use the entire sheet and draw where the water line is. On the tip of the iceberg, write *Anger*. On what is below the water, write feelings or situations that have hurt you in the past. Even if you believe you no longer feel the pain of these hurts, slights, embarrassments, or losses, write them anyway. Allow yourself to imagine what emotions you may connect with the situation and write those feelings. Allow yourself time for this exercise, and notice what feelings arise. Begin a plan on how to release those stored-up feelings. Will you hire a coach or get a trusted friend or therapist? Do you have a minister or rabbi you can turn to? This is your work and your responsibility.

TIERS OF HEALING II
SESSION 4: CHOICE

Do you know what happens when you give a procrastinator a good idea? Nothing!
—Donald Gardner

How soon, not now, becomes never.
—Martin Luther

Music Suggestion: "What One Man Can Do" by John Denver

What do you say you want? Take a moment and ask yourself how you want to feel, how you want to think, and how you want to respond to your life. Write your answers down. The choice is yours.

During the course of the day, we make hundreds of choices. Many of us were not taught how to make choices; we just made them. Some of us were not allowed to make choices; we came to believe that life just happened, and we had no say in what happened. Some people would rather do almost anything than have to make a choice of any kind. There is a good probability that these folks do not trust their own judgment.

Each of us was born with free will. We always have the choice to think whatever thoughts we want. What will you choose to think?

What do you want? What is one goal you would like to achieve? What one behavior do you have a desire to acquire or get rid of? Write what you want on a piece of paper. Keep this piece of paper close at hand.

Very often our higher power will give us a glimpse or a longing to change an aspect of our lives. Perhaps it is as simple as getting to bed at a more productive time or as complex as desiring to move to a different part of the country. We have this longing—this desire—and our internal chatter shuts the dream down as quickly as it appeared. Our beliefs may tell us, "No one in our family has ever lived in the West." Old, worn-out behaviors may shout, "If we go to bed at eleven, we will miss Jay!" Feelings can also take over: "You need to stay right here; Tim would have wanted you to stay here and be safe. You will be all alone and afraid and seven hundred miles from his grave!" Our self-talk robs us of our choices.

Many would argue that they choose to stay put, get little sleep, eat five thousand calories a day, or hold on to the pain they are experiencing. This is what they want to do. They may argue they want to be thinner, be happier, be healthier, yet their actions belie their statements. Know that it is your choice. You have free will.

Get the piece of paper on which you wrote what you longed for, what you wanted. Now, on this same piece of paper, write down all the feelings, thoughts, beliefs, and behaviors that keep you from what you say you want. If you are uncertain as to what is keeping you from what you say you want, take a moment or a day and declare what you want out loud. Notice your thoughts, your body sensations, and your past habits that have kept you from other dreams. Write them down. You will be using this list in the exercises for this session.

All human beings have choices. We may not have a choice about situations or governments or even if we are imprisoned, but we *always* have a choice as to what thoughts we will choose to dwell on. Pain is inevitable—all humans suffer pain and loss. Misery is an option. What choices will you make to move out of misery?

Exercises: Session 4

Supplies Needed: List from this reading, a few 3x5 cards, pen, marker, Journal or paper

1. Write what you most want on a 3x5 card. Use the words **I choose** _____ and fill in the rest (for example, "I choose to find a social group I like, to meet with weekly.") Use a dark pen or marker so the words are easy to see. Put this 3x5 card on your mirror. For one week, read the words aloud. Use a strong and clear tone. Do this at least once a day—twice is better.

2. After the week is complete, write down a belief, a thought, a feeling, and a behavior that keep you from what you say you choose (for example, There are no social groups for people my age—belief; I am so busy with work I do not have time—thought; I hate meeting new people, and I never know what to say—feeling; I procrastinate about searching Meetup.com to find groups—behavior).

3. It is now time to argue with your beliefs, thoughts, feelings, and/or behaviors. You may begin this by speaking aloud your argument as to why the thought, feeling, etc., is of little value, or is a lie, or no longer serves you. Keep your focus on what you are longing to choose as you argue your point.

4. Write down the results of your arguments. The goal of this entire exercise is to show you how you have choices and you have power. Make your choice—act.

TIERS OF HEALING II
SESSION 5: DOES THE PAST EQUAL THE FUTURE?

Without uncertainty and the unknown, life is just the stale repetition of outworn memories.
You become the victim of the past, and your tormentor today is yourself left over from yesterday.
—Deepak Chopra from *The Seven Spiritual Laws of Success*

Music Suggestion: "The Way We Were" by Alan Bergman and Marilyn Bergman

Healing a current wound and accepting what life looks like today very often require cleaning up past hurts and past losses that were not dealt with or swept under the rug. For the thousands of people we have worked with, the vast majority is not only suffering the loss of today, they are suffering the losses of decades ago. For some individuals, the feelings they have from a time when a parent left or a family pet was killed are just as real today as they were forty years ago. What these people were unaware of was the grief they still carried exacerbated their current grief. Healing is not an option—it must be done. If ignored or denied, grief will reappear again and again until fully accepted and healed. No one likes to hear these words, but we believe they are true. We have dealt with our own unexpressed pain and the buried pain of others for a combined total of seventy years.

Looking at our past with integrity and truth is the key to ensuring that we will not make the same mistakes we have in the past. Looking at our past with gentleness and love will ensure we will have the tools to heal our hearts now and release the hurts of yesterday. As Dr. Phil so often states, "You can't change what you don't acknowledge."

This session asks that we look at our past mistakes and behaviors, the qualities that did not serve us, and the wounds we ignored. It is *not* an exercise for beating yourself up or reviewing long-ago regrets. We are simply asking that your eyes are wide open and looking through the lens of truth. Once known, once acknowledged, our past can actually serve us, not hinder us. We may choose to take the best parts forward and dispose of all that no longer serves us today.

Dragging along past hurts, regrets, shame, and losses can weigh us down and sap us of our energy. To face forward, accepting what is today, takes strength and vital energy. Once we are able to release the past, our load becomes lighter and our future easier to envision.

Exercises: Session 5

Supplies Needed: Lined paper, crayons, a small lunch bag, soft music, and a candle

1. Begin by taking the time to list those losses from the past on a sheet of lined paper. Even if you believe you have healed from them, please list them anyway.

2. Next, list any hurts that may still be in your awareness and any shame you may have from past behaviors or actions. List any guilt concerning what you may have done or failed to do. Allow enough time in a place of quiet to be in total truth and integrity with this exercise. Allow yourself to go far back into childhood, listing names that still haunt you, abuses you felt or were a part of, anything that surfaces. Ask your psyche to share with you what you most need to release. You may be surprised by what surfaces. Write it down anyway.

3. Once you have listed anything and everything you would like to get rid of from your past, read over the lists. Notice any emotions you may still have regarding what you have written. List those old emotions. They have served you long enough; you may now release them.

4. If you would like to draw what you most want to release, this can be very powerful, as our right brain works with images and the left with words. When you combine both pictures and words, the results have more power.

5. Take a deep breath and put on soft music, light a candle if you wish, and create a prayer of release. It need not be long—a simple "Oh, God, I release all my past hurts, shame, and feelings to You. I no longer want or need them. Amen" will do.

6. As you say the prayer, begin to rip the lists you have created into small strips of paper. Crumble the papers and place them in the paper lunch bag. On the outside of the bag, write *garbage* or *trash*.

7. You may now bury this bag of garbage, or you may throw it away. Some people burn it in the fireplace.

8. Once you are finished, allow yourself a time of quiet reflection. Journal any feelings you are experiencing, knowing that your past does not need to equal your future.

TIERS OF HEALING II
SESSION 6: WHO IS RESPONSIBLE?

IT IS NEVER MY RESPONSIBILITY TO:
Give what I really don't want to give
Sacrifice my integrity to anyone
Do more than I have time to do
Drain my strength for others
Listen to unwise counsel
Retain an unfair relationship
Be anyone but exactly who I am
Conform to unreasonable demands
Be one-hundred-percent perfect
Follow the crowd
Submit to overbearing conditions
Meekly let life pass me by
It is never my responsibility to give up who I am to anyone
For fear of abandonment

Music Suggestion: "Responsible" by Leki

The process of acceptance involves taking a good look at responsibility. According to the dictionary, responsibility means fulfilling a duty or obligation. Responsibility does not include blame or guilt. When an individual is blaming or pointing a finger, he or she is not taking responsibility for their life.

Taking responsibility does not mean a person was not wronged or victimized. Pick up any daily newspaper, and it is obvious that there are people who prey on others. Events, experiences, and situations may not be of our own making; however, our reaction to said events is our responsibility.

Owning our feelings, our thoughts, and our actions is taking responsibility for our own life. Being overly responsible for others may make us feel good, but often it is a "heroic distraction" that keeps us from addressing our own lives. As we look at acceptance, it is a perfect time to determine on what side of the responsibility continuum we fall. Are we overly responsible—taking care of everyone regardless of age, keeping everyone happy, believing that tasks that could be shared are ours alone? Or under-responsible—blaming others for our own internal feelings, feeling victimized months after an event occurred, procrastinating on taking steps to move forward in life? The knowledge of where we are on the responsibility scale allows us to take the responsibility to shift.

Being overly responsible drains us. It is impossible to make everyone happy all at the same time. Taking responsibility for another's life (obviously this doesn't include children; we must be responsible for our children) limits the person's growth. It states to the universe: "This person cannot be trusted." Allow adults to be responsible for their own lives. They will grow, and you will have more energy to take responsibility for your life.

When we do not take responsibility for our own lives, we put ourselves in a place of victimization. Once we take back responsibility, we can make the necessary changes or additions to improve our lives and our thoughts. We think approximately sixty thousand thoughts per day. It is our responsibility to choose which thoughts we will follow and which ones we will let go. We have the ability to decide what we will accept.

Responsibility for your own life is a gift, not a curse. We are the captains of our ship, and knowing we have the choice of where that ship will go is part of the joy of living.

Exercises: Session 6

Supplies Needed: Journal, pen and paper

On a piece of paper, answer the following questions:

1. What am I trying to control in my current situation?
2. What is it I wish could be different?
3. If I could change one thing, what would it be?
4. How am I holding myself hostage in my current situation?
5. What is my payoff by staying in this situation and not taking responsibility to change it?
6. Make a list of all you cannot change and control (this is what you are not responsible for).
7. Make a list of all you can change and control (this is what you are responsible for).

TIERS OF HEALING II
SESSION 7: WHO DO YOU WANT TO BE?

It's a sad day when you find out that it's not accident or time or fortune but just yourself that keeps things from you.
—Lillian Hellman

Music Suggestion: "Scarlet Ribbons" by Jim Reeves

As we move toward an acceptance of our current situation, we begin to have a sense of who we want to be as we leave who we were behind. Who we are as individuals is made up of beliefs. Our beliefs shape our opinions of ourselves, the way we conduct our lives, the way we see the world, and the way we see others. When we change our beliefs, we are literally able to change our lives.

There is a true story about a man who climbed into a refrigerated train car to sleep. The door closed behind him and locked. Panicked, the hobo began to write on the inside of the refrigerated car that he was certain to die. He eventually died, and when the train car was unlocked, the man was dead of hypothermia. His belief is what killed him, as the refrigeration system was not working. The man believed he would freeze to death, and he did. This is an extreme example of the power of belief, but our beliefs are often so ingrained in us that we do not even recognize that it is possible to change them. We believe our belief set to be the only thing that is true of us and the world around us.

Beliefs can be changed. Remember, we have the right to choose. A significant loss has the power to reshape our world. Often the loss is in direct opposition to a belief we may have had. As our world is turned upside down, our beliefs may change on a subconscious level, leaving us disempowered...or, we may make the decision to change the belief and live our lives according to a new and more rewarding set of beliefs.

It is fairly easy to see what you believe and what others believe. Look at your life: if you are growing, healing, accepting, and taking responsibility, you believe in the power of your spirit to heal. On the other hand, if you are living a hand-to-mouth existence, devoid of any happiness or joy, you most likely believe in poverty of the soul.

Who would you like to be? Do you want to shift careers, eventually find love again, return to school, live with dignity and courage? Do you want to feel alive again and have the ability to laugh and feel grateful? Our inner beliefs shape our outer world. In order to change our beliefs and change our world, we must first recognize what we believe.

Look around your life, and with honesty and interest, jot down what someone might decide you believe. Do you follow your Self-Care Contract and keep your living space and car in good order? Do you say no when you know the request will keep you away from your healing journey? Do you spend time studying and learning? If the answer is yes, then someone may say that you believe you are important. Do you spend long hours away from home involved in career and advancement, rarely seeing your children? You may say you believe in family, but your actions say you believe in career advancement. Happiness comes when we live in alignment with what we say we believe. We are in harmony.

Our beliefs are typically formed at a very young age. There are four legs that go into building a belief table. The first may be a fact or an interpretation of a fact. It is something that happened (for example, our mother died when we were seven). The next leg is a powerful emotion that fills us (for example, the fear that no one would care for us). The third leg involves powerful sensory stimuli (for example, we heard adults crying, and we heard our father say, "I don't know how I will care for all of them"), and we then have this situation of fear that no one will care for us show up again and again (for example, our father forgets to send lunch money, no one remembers to check if our shoes are too small, and so on). We then form the belief at an unconscious level that no one will care for us. As we grow older, our belief that no one will care for us is lived out as we find people who we can care for instead, or we ignore our needs. We marry individuals who are intent only on their needs and forget about us. Beliefs are fascinating, and they are very, very powerful.

Decide now what empowering belief you would like to have. An example might be "People care for me and help me." Write it down. Now begin to dismantle your old belief ("No one cares for me"). You must allow time to notice how the belief you formed may have been true for a period of time, but it is not an absolute. If there are people you can find who do care for others (you may be one of those people), then it is possible for that to be a fact. Write it down. Allow yourself, through your imagination, to experience a strong emotion of what it would feel like to be cared for. Write or journal about what the feeling or feelings are. Now allow yourself to imagine what a person who cared for you would say—what would they whisper to you; how would they smile; what would they do for you? Would they touch you in a gentle way? Allow yourself to use the gift of imagination to fully experience what would happen and how it would feel. Now repeat this again and again. Spend time on this important belief-shattering and belief-building exercise. It has been proven to work time and time again.

There are no exercises for this session. Please spend your time with the lesson. Be certain to write down your thoughts and beliefs (new and old).

TIERS OF HEALING II
SESSION 8: FORGIVENESS

Forgiveness Affirmation:
I am releasing myself from all the demands and
Judgments that have kept me limited. I am allowing
Myself to go free—to live in joy and love and peace.
I allow myself to create fulfilling relationships,
To have success in my life, to experience pleasure, to know that I am worthy and deserve to have
What I want. I am now going free and in that process, I am releasing all others to be free.
I am forgiving myself, and I forgive them.
And so it is. And it is so.
—Adapted from an unknown author

Music Suggestion: "The Grudge" by Alanis Morissette

Forgiveness during a time of devastating loss may be the hardest thing any of us has ever done. It may also be the most healing action we can take. This one act alone may allow us to move powerfully into the future, leaving the past to memory only. Oprah once said, "Forgiveness is giving up the hope that the past could be any different."

Forgiveness never means forgetting or condoning who or what has hurt us. Forgiveness allows us to accept that we will try to learn the skills to lessen the chance that this hurt will happen again.

Forgiveness is not for the other person. Forgiveness is for us. Forgiveness allows us to move forward and not remain stuck in the past. Forgiveness is also not about denying our feelings of anger, resentment, or bitterness. These are normal feelings, and it is important to deal with them before attempting the process of forgiveness.

Forgiveness is not a process that happens overnight. It may take time and may happen in small steps and stages. Take your time. You may not want to forgive; that is your choice. When I was going through a significant betrayal and divorce, it became my prayer to be willing to want to forgive. I did forgive and am at peace. It took several years and much prayer and coaching, but I knew that my only path to joy was through forgiveness. There is a saying that holding a grudge is like drinking poison and expecting the other person to die. Forgiveness is for your soul, your spirit, your healing.

Forgiving before you are ready is what Debbie Ford calls putting ice cream on poop. Graphic, but true.

Often we need to also forgive ourselves. We will come back to forgiveness in future Tiers, but you may do the process on yourself now if you so wish.

Be gentle as you go through this process. You may take as much time as you wish. Remember, it took me years. In order to truly forgive, you must be willing to feel the pain that you are forgiving. Please remember this process is for you. You may never hear an apology for the pain you experienced. The person or people involved may believe they were in the right. Forgive to let go, and move on. As long as you are caught in the web of bitterness and hurt, you are being held back from the life you could be living.

Life is too short and too precious to waste being stuck in the muck of blame. Forgiveness begins with a decision to not punish ourselves for the wrongs or the circumstances that occurred and to move on to a life full of love and joy. There is hope.

Exercises: Session 8

Supplies Needed: Forgiveness Contract, paper, pen, envelope, stamp

1. Make a list of everyone you need to forgive. Decide whom you are willing to forgive. Put those names in the Forgiveness Contract that follows.
2. Write a letter of forgiveness from your heart and place it in a sealed envelope. Mail it to yourself and then allow it to be in the special area that you have set aside in which you do this work, if you so decide.

Forgiveness Contract

I, _____, choose to stop punishing myself and feeling hurt for what (list names below) has done. I release them and accept I am unable to change the past.

Signed_____ Date_____

Be grateful that you don't already have everything you desire.
If you did, what would there be to look forward to?
Be grateful when you don't know something,
for it gives you the opportunity to learn.
Be grateful for the difficult times. During those times you grow.
Be grateful for your limitations,
because they give you the opportunities for improvement.
Be grateful for your mistakes. They teach you valuable lessons.
Be grateful when you are tired and weary,
because it means you have made a difference in the world.
It's easy to be grateful for the good things.
A life of rich fulfillment comes to those
who are also grateful for the setbacks.
Find a way to be grateful for your troubles,
and they can become your blessings.
—Author Unknown

Music Suggestion: "Let Out the Joy" by Peter Schroeder

We believe that the doorway to joy is gratitude. Having an attitude of gratitude is a healthy way of beginning the healing process. During times of grief and healing, it may be difficult to find something to be grateful for, and it is exactly at those times it is necessary to search for what to put on a gratitude list.

For many of us, when we are in pain, all we can see are the negative aspects that caused the pain in our lives. We begin to focus on the negative, trying desperately to fix things, struggling to make things better at the expense of not noticing all that we have to be grateful for in the moment. We wear ourselves out with worry to the point where some of us are too exhausted to focus on all the positive things we may have in our lives. For some, the positive may be difficult to find, but there is always at least one thing to have gratitude for each day.

Gratitude puts us in touch with the power of the universe and introduces us to a new way of looking at faith and God. God is the benevolence and love of the universe. God's gifts are always within our reach. It is up to us to open our hand and receive whatever gifts or blessings the day has given us.

We do not profess to say this is easy. There are days that gratitude is difficult. Often, by asking the question, "What could I be grateful for today?" we are able to begin the process of gratitude. Allowing yourself to find at least one thing to truly feel grateful for has the ability to move you from despair to hope. As you continue expanding your field of gratitude, you may find yourself at the door of joy, a place you did not realize you could find. Gratitude provided the path. Make it a part of your life from today going forward.

Exercises: Session 9

Supplies Needed: Paper and pen, Journal, candle, an open mind

1. Begin your day, before you get out of bed, by asking yourself, "What can I find today to be grateful for?"

2. During your day, notice what shows itself to you. It may be the buds of spring, the sun shining through the windows, a beautiful sunset. Perhaps you can be grateful for your ability to smile at a stranger. Make a game of gratitude, and look at least hourly for what brings gratitude to your heart.

3. Begin to make a list of all that you are grateful for. You may include the past and the present. Include childhood memories, favorite places, friends, and even foods you love. Take one week and write down all that comes to you. At the end of the week, take time to read through the list. Allow yourself a time of quiet. Put on the suggested music, perhaps light a candle, and read the list you have created. As you read the words, allow an image to form in your imagination. Take some time to feel the gratitude entering your heart and then slowly move to the next item on your list. Take your time. You may notice emotions rising—this is normal. Stay with your list. Use your breath to move through your emotions and allow the gratitude to build and begin to feel the joy of being alive. You are accepting, and there is hope.

TIERS OF HEALING II
SESSION 10: HONORING YOURSELF

People may ask you, "How do you know God?"
You should respond, "Because He is my Heart."
Can we know ourselves if we do not know God?
The real understanding of ourselves is our understanding of God.
—Persian Wisdom

Music Suggestion: "How Could Anyone" by Libby Roderick

Seldom do we take time to honor ourselves and who we are at the deepest level of our being. When we were growing up, we often heard phrases such as "Don't get too big for your britches," "Don't get a big head," "Stop bragging," "Who do you think you are?" or "What is the matter with you?" I'm sure you can add many more to this list. As children, we took these criticisms to heart and stopped acknowledging ourselves as the unique beings we are.

We have been created as spiritual beings having a human experience. We are created in the image of God. Our Higher Power has gifted us with our own unique gifts, which are designed to bring the world something that it so badly needs. Only you have the secret to what those gifts are. Some of you know what your gifts are and are able to accept them as valuable. For some, you have left it up to others, such as family and friends, to catch a glimpse of your gifts. Whatever the case, it is time to show the outside world your gifts.

Honoring yourself at the deepest level may bring up some uncomfortable feelings such as embarrassment, shame, shyness, and invisibility. Humanity needs each and every one of our gifts. It is important to move past any feelings of inferiority that may arise. If you find it difficult to honor yourself for your own benefit, please do it for the world.

In Tier I, we asked all participants to buy or make a beautiful box. In this box, they could place all their items that they wanted to be acknowledged for or gave them a sense of pride. If you do not have an acknowledgment box already, it is time to get one now. Your self-care involves self-acknowledgment and a time of deep honoring.

We honor all who have the courage and commitment to move from a place of despair to a new reality. You have moved through grief and have now come to a place of acceptance. Please contact us if you have any comments or questions.

Exercises: Session 10

Supplies Needed: Paper, pen, envelope, stamp, creative mind, a mirror, acknowledgement box

1. This is very important to do. Take the time and write yourself a letter listing what you honor yourself for. Write the letter as if you were writing about some other person. An example might be:

Dear Susan,

I want to honor you for your enormous courage this past year. You have maintained such integrity as you have gone through the layoff at work. You were able to help others with their feelings of loss as you upheld your own work ethic and continued working as if your job would last for another ten years. You have faced the future with hope, despite your age and the current economy. Susan, you are a hero in my eyes. I honor you for all you have done and all that you are.

In Gratitude,
Your #1 Fan

Once you have completed this letter, wait three days and mail the letter to yourself. When you receive the letter, schedule a time to read it. You will need a mirror, as you are going to read the letter aloud and look into your eyes as you read. Read a few words, and then look in the mirror and say the words again, letting them sink deeply into your heart. Continue this until you have completed the entire letter. Now, put the letter in your acknowledgement box and date it.

2. Decide what you would do for a person you wanted to honor. Would you send her flowers? Take him to dinner? Bring her a gift and sit with her? Decide what you would do, and then do that for yourself. **Be certain that whatever you decide to do that you share why you are doing that particular action with whomever you come into contact.** For example, if you order flowers for yourself, inform the order taker that you are doing this to honor yourself. This may feel uncomfortable. Do it anyway.

3. Give yourself a hug, and tell yourself how amazing you are. We believe you are amazing and would love to hear from you!

anne@tiersofhealing.com

You have completed Tier II, *Journey to Acceptance*. Congratulate yourself on moving through this difficult Tier. As you encounter struggles in the future, use your knowledge and skill at accepting the unacceptable. Remember, the pain is in the resistance to what is (as Debbie Ford stated again and again).

Remember, also, once we accept where we are and what is facing us, we then have the power to act. Using our power and life force to go back in time is senseless and robs the world of our unique contribution. Acceptance is not condoning.

We are here to serve you and support your journey. We have walked the path of resistance and have the scars to show for our struggle. Our hand is offered that your journey may be easier and filled with the Light that is available to us all.

May you continue on your path with joy,
Anne